FIRST NETTLES

FIRST NETTLES

Dom Hale

The Last Books   Amsterdam/Sofia   2025

For Viola and Amelia

The world is a theorem that nobody wants to prove anymore, and I have the feeling the sacred places of the earth are burning before my eyes.
 —Jean Daive

Everybody says I'm wrong.
 —Dean Blunt

Walked I know not where.
 —Dorothy Wordsworth

1

Your Auspice 13
For Mau 14
Song: North Sea 16
Comfort Zone 17
Go on Then 19
Reef Time from Tim's Reading 20
Song: Groundsel 21
In the Scratching Shed 22
Fashionably Late 26
Link Rot 27
Wandering Light 28
Reply to Sam After the Heatwave 29
A Dedication for Trench Foot 31
Parole 33
Decade of Innards 35
Purgatory for Angels 36
Hedge Accentor 38
Doing Numbers 40
Misrule 41

2

Paroxysm: A Strain 49
Went Whistle 50
A History of Birdsong 51
For the Ones that Care 52
Patent 55
Rufford Park Poachers 56
Song: Lung Bud 57
Market Psychology 58
Thermal Storage 60
Giving Back 61
The Servant and the Stick 62
Castor and Pollux 63
Song: Mire Drum 66
Cockatrices and Echoes 67

Human Factors 68
State Funeral 69
Plaque's Heap 70
Lug Poem 73
Visual Snow 74
War Blur 75
Unnumbed 77
Herne the Hunter 79
Hymn from Careers 81

3

Crude Thoughts 87
A Salamander 90
The End of Melancholia 91
Muck for May Day 94
Water and Armour 95
Ode to Spit 98
I Love to Walk the Fields 101
Aureole 103
Seizures 104
Viewless 115
Coupon 116
After and Before 118
Changing the Guards 120
Song: Emissions Cap 121
Interregnum 122
My Shadow 123
First Nettles 127
Instead of Sleep 128
Crown Shyness 129

Index of Titles and First Lines 135
Acknowledgements 139

ONE

YOUR AUSPICE

    The wing is an anvil. Kevlar the sunset, existence
            and recreation, now our minute shifts bitterly
                        in the hacked light of the stock exchange.
              No sudden grief, no great tragedy to sweep
us off our feet and into an unnerving evening
            knowing sorrow and amazement and difficulty.
                    Not even my sold salute.

But truth travels secretively on. Only this inhospitable earth
        where the sight of somebody enjoying themselves
                for longer than it takes to mix a cocktail
           is enough to send the harriers over the brink.
How mountainous the petrol-crashed
      graph of the city,
                        the music you follow to its vanishing point.

FOR MAU

listen to the falconet   haar-fold
in an overgrown garden
              hemmed snow grey by blocks
to pulling my shirt off the cord

                the skull's a cavity
that proves something
among sharks   & legal skyline
so that the world nearly forgets us

and polar suicide
cracks open   shell of a walnut
is gone

    what defence does a poet have?
redwing slingshot
              pings from thought branches

I've stood in rooms been flanked
by slat numb sunlight
                useless drunk

it's that things fall away from me
ambitions for songs
         until I know less
than a blowtorch   confidence
              of milling about
saughton walls
and there are hardly any words to carry us

         how I reach out of the whirlpool
that abyss. with one last job for prometheus

what jetty will art have?

if suffering bluff-sways, and the administrator
types out a chain

but they won't buy us   no shoal to
they won't.
gold gale
                    flash fire
                                offices go up
my name is not my name

SONG: NORTH SEA

you've been a loner on the earth
gulls know what I'm about

costume, grass style, shallows
great grandparents of the factories

this is not a poem
poems are for the management

a fleeing noise
how do you fake that

COMFORT ZONE

left the openair bathhouse   sauna to sand martin
    poetry is dead. long live poetry

when we're really having to fend for ourselves here
        tortoiseshells   dragged grimly along
          a wraith gummed to a tablet

impossible to 'administer' the revolt from above
                        like a clever prescription
    outlined tasteful as Ricard on
           Fitzcarraldo coffee table

        but be canny & nimble, patient
under the mead-gold dusk
                          keeping both lugholes out

    exterior speech gone from us for a long bloody time
bitter pall & shade, collective lyric
            the swivel of lockdowns   drift losses
      to scumbag vacuum

and sick as a collared dove
                        or Chanticleer
    annoying southern fens
                with hundredth squawk
                    a bare yieldful of boke

I realise statues were fringing me   corral frack toll
        and the slalom had greater magnitude
    than marmoreal air   slipping down
                            pitcher plant oesophagus
          another shot, extra ice & tabasco

see I've never felt more lethargic in my life
                        and more resolve
    youre almost everything that's heard

                    grey photo of Taylor, Lord
fed pigeons on the smashed roof of Strangeways

    or John Ball
              Blackheath fugitive
or Sophie summoning ghosts
    in the bigger shadow   of Strata SE1
      destroys their ringworm seclusion

got to push that energy around I think
    no more slumped by a PC on the edge
              or not only

   in leisurely state slaughter   kick cordoned off, joke coterie
      that type of stent
quartered as a lesson to the rest of the livestock

    but vitalitys pressure
        our epithets   titles are yours
   our best lines, dimmed worlds wheel off

to rend & invent
        to pleat & flow
   my life known freely
              my life unmade

GO ON THEN

a horse-dart over the silo leads
to the sense of falling foul of
ember syllables
somewhere close by, an electric
blanket pulsing through midwinter
as the unbuilt way I
ripple between panes, acts, tell me
maybe we're not always our arguments

and what we'll do is walking intervals
in meaninglessness, from the role plinth
from crosstalk like a trick of the banks
automated threats give
bailiffs cloud cover
because to be cold is
civilising, unbreakable paperwork
nailed to this eluding street

did professionals often
teach you to kill? is
jealousy a principle
in the gift sky-jaw? just bring bits
& hoof it, realising the mountain
disappears exactly
at every cairn
you have nothing to announce but the altitude

REEF TIME FROM TIM'S READING

last defiance is a deep landscape so my hearers taught me

the word ones walkie-talkieing
through pal-glow flightpath

        conscripted country mouse
whorls over a moss metier
more horizontal, seers emptying the carton lane

a helper, awkward
        from delay, next
the factory for spotless parts
we wrote down in aprils dream journal
                then that tock radiance is a task

it arises in several gnarled forms
    doesnt belong to trappers
and no one happy or well pays any attention

bleached out scales must moved to a necrotic
city like all the tethered others

to recover an old shoelace & weathercock, disgusted at these times
        the mouth harp barely broke on us

but poetry isnt only its survival
head sanded in burials
            wraith chipper
wracks torture's source
and the halfpolitics of a secret, unassimilable storybook

your good ear's paintbrush
hushing the firm armaments of gods

now I'll level with the evil chiffchaffs everywhere
I saw
one swear

SONG: GROUNDSEL

a twist of the syllable, the billed spirit
beneath investment
number reins

I go out to the woods, done love
is an ear
heard in the cruel dirt

shallow parts, hears where
a constellation roots you
canvas over us

the naming ends, a jet
breaks in the ribcage
it gives onto impossible

IN THE SCRATCHING SHED

    And handled with a Chain –
       —Emily Dickinson

    There must be something more than this mere settling
    for a history of resilient feelings.
       —Stephen Rodefer

I keep green wits about me
                          turp return
    to the blade basement & burn a coronet

all the slogans err, calming cages

              so I shatter my growth
& submit to nerve movement

undictated through pterodactyl aerospace
written oily, slowly off

              watch spoke pressure
                    swap our pasts for a blocked shrine

only attitudes   to itch in the strait.

      but you didnt give up on us if I cross
                          the laplake street
motion says clone sales are sedated

              and the nearest rook woods

       where I've gone to grapple
a full-faltering middle name   avoided void

   away to find out something for ourselves.

dehydration of one personal ache   yet it tarred
                     selfharm on recursive suburbs

thought we couldnt desire to boss

							any flung body, slicing apart

				whats individual where you tarn-build

		tethersong of the depressions
										shed its hind legs

and a daily practice of crossed generousness
					sharpens poems on your dozing elbow.
I forget most of the little french I had.

			how to understand this crime of boredom
						on crumbling plane of seamless entertainment

alloyed with the most terrible shit youve seen
not a dirk in waiting

			wiggle tomb					big like our deckedout sky
compassion as a last defense

from insulated saints whove got a problem with whatever shimmy
						lolled by their shared bank account

			antitank imagination
						splutters on the tablecloth.

to perform a dummy disappearing act
			when aid was hunted

							rams reprimand
emotional battlements

			withdrawal like the busted totem.

no wish to participate, daring never
		again		never fought to compete

					only save some necks & blowback
			if a hungry vineyard tonguebird
						(I hate rhetoric as well)

(thank fuck noone reads these)

			and as the streaming colonnade lives estrangement
						the den was the algorithm

    still prophecy carves its own deadend.

              like a kind of love can derail toe-thought
it has its paradox   fables & footholds of winterkill.

to write as one of the least
            hardy creatures in the workingworld

swinging between poles
                with unearned lick luck

    and to do it because of
                          not in spite of this marred reality
       but refuse to be literal   about snared asthmatic breaths

a poets only public is the wind.

              to be really of the march
a craving to just narrate your
late clashed tyro history turns to sand

                the proofer gets the slip
        you feel along the thread to the blood-brain barrier

dying hermit homes inward deeply
                            to sweep out glitter-arc.

           where monuments cave in.

my single errand now is like upwards rain off mouse-ear
                          the floating lute
   in war tempo

           a cursor over our flexible heads

cling to your eviction   wolfish
               become an outer foil

        and under an aurora anyone
                will stop hurting themselves

as intentions fade into the cursed valley
                corpse of 'international law'
   a fake election called through sheetmetal

low teeter form   so lets persist & bedraggle
                    our own sepal cities

glad to make social stoat
                disharmony for good

raged lint lilac

tripping skewly back north
            which is impelled curds, purposeless & wounds

                            so that paranoia converts to a guising lighter

            in unclear flow, stay weirdo
                                            but range your forward spots

shift on shift   nil fluttering off into a cosy
                    nuclear future

        O red fend

what if the brimming
                        hedgerow kept us mapped

FASHIONABLY LATE

The rockdove at the end of the palace coos
I will never be beautiful.

To flee-fear things & love them at once.

Landscapes stress out.
The internet has tortured
you into a fleck worth something.

New stage of art
open in sunleap lasso, it cheats me. The costumer
is always right.

Warehouse, will we rustle.

Seacoast, sole traders
are flying about like songbirds.

But I required you back in the door
of the season, little knave,

to break the sound barrier,
scared of sounding
like myself.

Money's the weakest seeing there is.

Little night, I'm off
under that snapdragon atmosphere.
Don't say this is too much like poetry.

A dipped
star winks for chasm absence only. Ah,
Mephistopheles.

LINK ROT

Move on the hinge. You think a composer
presence we make of each other
is about PR
the filament of monarchies & salesmen
getting their moneys worth out of the wide berth.
It's been possible to speak sprawl lawed
A planet in the vial.
Guessing to invent new manoeuvres
or tap into the sound spree, needing to retrieve it
from the jaws of academicism
crevasse polysyllables, is this what you wanted to hear.
That the birds don't
believe a thing I say. Thousands of empty flights
to preserve slots, an electric fence
forgets the form of the poem.
Afternoon, pluperfect. Junked
by then.
Too warm, too rushed
plant-based constellations
kicking above a startup, hiding in tongues
between this display
& this display.
A 'lower income patient'. A
rook tirade. You
come to the balcony of it
seeing Gazprom in the instant in the silence. And when the nice kids
who went to certain schools
command poems
At the limit, toting
My loyaltys
not to the
saved

WANDERING LIGHT

June wooze
levered me out of sleep paralysis
reading your hermit crab, there when it was needed

finest star is this one & the ground we're at
a new space race vampirism

like I don't always get what our poems are for exactly
but there's the extent, this sort of stealing out
infinity's floret
in slant broom, to the off-path people

shucked shellseeking by the seashore
we don't watch our words

or songs against themselves, turned in, hallucinating impossible real violence
hatred of the owners of time
I need them

and in the draughts of the world night
around with these slugs you actually give a shit about, one noise
I need this too

ignore the expiration date
made up by a machine
controlled by bureaucrats & the corporation brains
tastes alright still doesn't it

REPLY TO SAM AFTER THE HEATWAVE

All over the scar water, shaped ex-
        plosions of seabirds
bone-colour gannets & multipointed terns
My existence nearly unfrozen, upturned on the ridge
      my pinnacle of scant thoughts
              that I bring through spore song
here in the mixer, tapestries of
CFO dust, hangover sweat, joint fluff
              the cost of living
      and what that means, a buffed screen
a tongue briar lashing at the
      illuminated book, the long road to Red Tadcaster
          Saint Aidan, Saint Mutter, shit pixels
observing a grey squirrel going about stuff
            in somebody else's poem
under the skylark Internationale
love everywhere
      food must be stashed away for the winter
like a missing signature
    Pot Still minded in west coast cold.
When Jimmy Grove lies on his deathbed
      for love of Barbara Allen
           he is translated
      and eddying around us
commercial development of the Merz Barn
        your phone thats listening to you
    school pals who grew up, found jobs, bought cars
the collapse of a government but not an architecture
      because I wanted to try to dodge
          all the hungry naming
& inhumanity, a vital trowel put in my hand by the garden
the story of how we became poets
    though it's never the right temperature, boiling
hot or absolutely baltic, fucked—our friends
        bang on about timing & alertness
              and they're right too
the revolution in old songs, it's not transcendence
    The silver birch never burns out.

And the rime never gets finished
Sam ... we both understand that. Interruptions
   east & west, social poetry
      the bastardised forms, stoned
         & cackling, a stonechat
chats to cursed stones. It takes a good while to dam,
    to pick that many parsley leaves off the stalk
  the poets only light lamps
         before they vanish
so that I can't ever talk about logistics, not really, shelves
      turning bare
     the splint self goes, I pitch my tent
  head feels hollow
hazelnut shell. No way is it the best joke
       you've ever walked in to
  the tripod kicked over
    I get hitched to the poem, and the poem
kills me in return.
      Inscrutable flaming California
       the deaths of our parents,
lost in the news planet roster
the least of the moon, this fragment has one slice for me
        & one slice for you
   Gold chasm between terraces.
    My bus disappears.
In this acidic drain where money is freedom
       I bind myself to drifts of sky
  a breach in the dead heart that flowers.
The integrity of a single morning
    this single morning,
      bravery of a hand on the key

A DEDICATION FOR TRENCH FOOT

the voices fall on my ears from all tight angles
channel for skunked up rage
      gone apeshit

whats audible in the trance

weapon under scut wing
tech leaders waging foul laws
          kaleidoscopic blue pursuer

from Minch brawl in summerautumn
stank guga off the hunt pole

     cinquefoils
sharp as hailstorm

a hound chatting to hounds

and clouds so thick you can't see shoes

someone hands me a wrench
              another tells me I'm dead

light pact potless
calls our trellis hostile

but it's his mic
sounds like chain-link
      tourist shadowboxing

guess the county *artists* in this casket
are mostly frustrated politicians

rent stumped
from the paternal shares
              entrepreneur on vulture buttress

don't give it the time of day
boot the van

        horizon blows itself sky-high

I heard that

they're cooked

time is a bridle
           perennials echelons

and the incandescent
coalesces into the image
of the feather of
           a jay

PAROLE

deep memory
        unmurdered

    surround my set in battered noise
        I heard you

                walking out of the burning flats
    with no west frond

        left off red
        start wreckage

    edged lovely as day pared down
        its live ply dust

        sea speech
        buckthorn night task

knowledge lunged at the climate
        making chord muck

    beyond harvest mouse brackets
        pursuit of cuticle so built

                fresh air to billow bindweed
            went once through new wind

    in a lowlight landfill flare
my delta stutter

        silt altered by note-near
        slanging match

            torn from untimed tides
                policy stole shape

nicked inland moss under most blue
        made beck as I came back

    you for a curving cycle
              forced factory disasters

                        night but not eternally

that knife grout & a grapple shale riot
                asked everlasting growth

        half-accent, therefore
        of the worthless

                shade shoptalk, therefore
                          immortal air gulf

DECADE OF INNARDS

your overseers won't leave you to your writing
your writing won't leave you to yourself

PURGATORY FOR ANGELS

I woke up and the earth was still there.
by the tollhouse, robinlang

      out the half-shut mouth
of a little kid, that doesn't make sense to me, click-a-clay

leathered in kerosene. all these unfinished pieces.

         they crashlanded in a plane with their dad.

the poem says to be counterintuitive, the dinted willows show
(wile-willows)
millworker who abandoned the mill.

                how the atoms
                wend, partly, hyperhale to you

sprawl to a keystep, over on my head, trainers
like two questions to the abyssal
            troposphere

cos every day it accrues,   the
cash pressurelure, to make pigs out of pennedness
ourselves in drill-delving
        a set of explosions christened dominations

I didn't fancy summarising whatever some rep
thinks our 'problems' should be

         thats just journalism, its social work
one day the shaving mirror's got to be kicked in.

doublerainbow
description, critique even
        don't always scoot us away from the teachout

shits clear and no garlanding. else dug, king
saves a god, blanks me, streams

diversionary
winsome bubble, metamorphic beat

and in the same second ticked clarity bombs...
body armour, cams, faultline walk
I'm not trying to cope or
                      console. I won't care about the handsome.

now 'saviourism is kerb-ditching'
now 'the angle of inclination of his creatureliness'

english is horrible. but we can raze
heads w/ it, contort it using inlet farrago
jink on jink

contested air. tapehiss. your moves
                      respire in spiral fastness

teaching as a way to tread & wander
as a way to learn (sheerly) like a dead lang rings for you

so screw duty.
        it's the pourboire
        shatters
        gunmetal crossing, TV telos,   leave
                triumph to the conquerors.

was no miner, I piss about in frosty grass
cold quarry lakes
      indivisibly, off-root

that dizziness sends me
windchime back to others

                      it's the impasse hurls us
                            but we vamp

HEDGE ACCENTOR

flute inside how to not die down slowly
but achieve charms, purled, straddling the updraughts of the city
as you leave it behind

a big art life
spinning a denunciation a shepherd moon
chewing tobacco in mauled autumn
the least political of sore throats
'friends are the first to turn on you'

course I didn't get into this cloud thicket
to suss out predetermined problems, bird solves bird
once & for all
gone into the world of frostbite

stung way more crooked than that
the false sparrow's outrageous vow just north of the heart & lungs

in outcast darkness
late weimar terror
reedling sideways always

like back of abingdon market, chime
does uvula
tackiness was our aesthetic category
that and the leet wind off the steep sea

the statement in the poem
cut the noose, for an infinite millisecond
to be able to write again, overthrow the lifeguards
blue shit mica levi

because the powerlessness & embarrassment of a single life
gets bract transformed
on the pier, in the tip, with others quiet corolla

fastened from streaming
to put up undrownable reality, sky saplings, mud ramps
a scrape a plume a blown brick

as if the healed clown
could climb back into the trench

as if a poet
could pick their element

waif dawn. to have killed winter

DOING NUMBERS

so at first light there'll be a curve
we plant things, the city shoulders
no burden but what silhouettes give to it
thin reflections passing between cars & wind

you suffered in work
but didnt let it make you
wish others would suffer more in theirs
that, in its gapped way, was beyond
official grace & compassion
and secretly inside it, the nucleus
to blow the whole situation to pieces
torch shit, like a logic of the wayside

but what would that take
even the wintering thought of it, girders, sap
done in, what ace or poisonous sacrifice
the egos of small
people at war with each other for rubble
derailing any conduit
except stuff a fallow flame breaks out

nah, the long tube shudders
and beams from longdead stars
are startling, uncertain
this hilled language returns them

MISRULE

> Well how can that be fair at all
> —Talk Talk

Circling the square   it flick spoke like struck me
     you forge your own chatter
for gridiron surround soundings
Thats our corn language
            omadawn   yap yaffle, it's where
we feel brought, temp Stoke Newington sunspot
     Melodious scowl dusk peaks
                           in the deem drift
          consuming scales of murder
where formula airs end w a gasp   thorn northed
     in the footer, time to get off the internet you lot
Time was when stoked October
          together piss wet that mad cow
sin in the vale   freak'd
     tongue-and-eye trance like the only
                        cosmic vision of a long past
         oral tradition worth haggling with
hey presto
              so Avril bee
                      combs May Day
The rolling fields grow dark as the grave
Prefer this shadiness
             yen to steep across decoration
       winged stylus you indicated crated
                 behind winding copse
destroy the herder
        flame handle
     when I was sunk in soddening prosody
                    or down yon dowie den
In those heaven eras out of the flat took starrish nerve
whacked from hollow sociality in
       fantasy of the rightminded
              bought wings   got me back
Seek to do it all now weir ways
               necker guide

        dissolve us in usurpation fleshes, ouroboros
patience leads on to dandelion doolally
           glanceturned into a sandstone pillar
                      Will singe whiteheads, singe the
rich crowd, ruthless unit seraphim
first hint of psychic
          distress to be ditched, mockingbirdily
for the next rung   A flower juts onto
I take no ownership of just methods   is mask posy
undoing a talk as we grove go
           trio bluethroats unhanged in Angleterre
       innards doused to wreck & dust
and necropolis on ahead.
                        That the missiles fall nonspecifically
the slaughterhouse bil. songs most at home in
          paveway to stormshadow
to blessèd professional-
          ised iris   ay gloats madcapstone
                needs taunting
     amassing for institutional status
Lam that   noise us into the gutter loit
how not to shore up the catarrh, this
       vent sanction
              chimes hovelly   Tom Mann
countersinging from
     his bare anthill, link lost, doled through doldrumfire
Screen bills are great mimics
        have their xeriscape
in the well-copped ozone shield
I thanked everybody.   I always made
an awful bowsprit, regiments of
       slicks   delude them, deludding   I am
             upup over the heath shear sailing

The century is after us. It might be
     you dont ever find the love you crave in the exterior world
          subsecrecy & last impressions
poem builds it out for   dipped night naysaying
The life of one of us alone can't claim that
       reverence   dignified drey vantage
Yeah, youll finish the espresso
     yeah art's a setup
         but antelistening trills transformation
in the depths of forest
mumbling among 'entities'

                                    Who was I speaking at? Or to, even
Fen-feared
the foals of Agincourt. Moi. We solitary
                    route. Continuing chestnut
        to daub & drool   was touched
by presentmindedness
                            chronicle after the mushroom bothy
or wreak in tongues
            slash send a postcard
Now a world from our sponsors, your name for poison
        gift   presses for profit
flayed like a satyr
                    in the blanched corrie
Prussian
blue sky thought
Starbank Park attracted via
                giving music back to bloodletters
careering for fame
                while bird lips   streak stark news
The click upturns
                    in top-down swipe architecture. Got it.
Machine learning sly out-
sourced to ghosts
                    another term for live
I eat my offal
        composition on stolen time
                        vied offlane
Cry servants who won't transcend themselves
                                are setting awkward fires
escape in fabrication
        which is the same utensil as staying here holding your mum's head
Paradise—columbarium—city—wilderground.
            The street whips into its promise
                        and I don't only sketch, record it, exhibit
my ragged symptoms, but play a twin-wren part in the phenomena
        no less or more   reefed, measuring my
                        splitness in how we steal away &
                hide or cradle our own impasse
when it stings like fuck   stimrhythm for the unloved
        And soil latterly
                am I surviving a tortured lie
to 'shock the fantastic dictionary'
                        carbon clouds
sissonne in that unglamorousness
                        old dependency, knead-high skip

          as the functions start to fail
                but it isnt inevitable yet
and I don't have to do that   ach for my twitch couriers
      Spoon ran back with the dish
                killing competition in its fused heart
black hole flock
cos rhyme's a cloak to wash ensign bitters
                mountainous devildoubt
Will the aside float down
        on the ley, this countrys too sucked for us
Cold, massacred horizon
         A poet's technique
                is glacé-voiding
    sea ice note
          in commonplaces   chirrup hunger
I love Hyatt for writing no
              on the evenings I perceive it

A wicker cot missed by lightning
full of shit.
    The angel's role in enchainment
empyreal Pyrenees   burnt capped hearse
    heard empires collapse
        like jambs to the laughter
Amazon warehouse raked in dead light.
Which lingua franca I'm voicing now. Vague wand
      at the terminal moraine of Investopedia
  riotfeeder   blackberry stains on a tomb
      get fucking yeeted beyond solace in the reprisals.
I only twinge for myself   but am severe veering
    for the turnkey
w what the abyss speaks
a fleck desecration over true melos
    quiver among oblong
        constructions & the buds' brownfield.
At the antisolar point.
    And hey, kingdom delight
        is sea-surrendered since
gone Naples
        12hour monologue about your property
I wish it underwater
    jack in the summit   toll harlequin
      The future's risoed & pairs well with our tartare
Snare. Shack fit. Tilt
    zero consolation. No harmony of the provinces.

      Swan leaf is ecstatic.
Just the spectral
   shattertruth of my attacked corpsing, wage reptilian sky
tinctures the insane boomerang
I embrace to the remnant
      like a partner in time
          God bless thy lungs, goodnight

TWO

PAROXYSM: A STRAIN

This is the simplest poem
it is in me to make. The poets of us
never will unfurl defeat

Searching rotors
muntered cloudy
done beaut note
      kept last inside my hat

I walk-wander under a
wide iron heaven, regulatory heaven, the
humiliation of going to work for
someone you can't stand

Permanent residents
exercising their right of way
That old hunch
about being imperceptibly but systematically embalmed
      means abrupt and tulip-handed

Not for me, only I'm sidling
lupine, pint-minded
to a wrecking tune
becomes the most onerous thing

In Astor's icehouse, exchangeable
suits of the rulers

You turn on the smiling TV
and the president of the world is standing there to say
'thus far there has not been a significant overreaction'.

Tear it to the ground, it has to go forever
Run to your senses.

WENT WHISTLE

poetry sled out
where the gate lurk world interjected

scar slight trioleate
cockiness on sundial

                                            no fourth life
apple juice, twigged & said several footholds

got really into shallow breathing
door-door—drill town rode under

a scrape bird in urgency
                              approach shade, dodo, the world cones

see the heartburn feels good, ear-harsh
lossy daytime, tall turquoise seastack

fire now & beaut to cross over for
not missed mystified violets

        deliberate commission with a buried head
all work must meet it

each art wing
spoke

shall go unmiraculous
                          brush pens sharpening up

to turn a like line by
the by of our errors

the icon with net taste
        airs me under the goat willow

A HISTORY OF BIRDSONG

                                        temp sky
like willowware with blood streaks

appeases nothing
        I took a filed tare in the mark burgh

Puck peeking through quickset
to ignite barrier   *carry here*

a thought of earthshine
                out stockade of politics
                                        ruthless nape-knock
I heard from a scop's earring

separating dead from the chaff

                        duskworker

mistreating of instruments
to morph feelings over   (morphed, think)

        a hem remedy
        remiges

snuck lint and dinted the weather carving
above blue kyle

thieved

                        was a heath goldsmith
hiding from the beak
                                  did it also mean
                                  fief   chiff

            becoming hidden from each other

FOR THE ONES THAT CARE

    Memory should agitate
      —June Jordan

Never a night as flawless as it is out here
lit joint, pink smudges   city lane
         dusk-dragged
warble fording sound
against traffic's part-silence
I've not been, I won't
         ever work over myself.
To be held by the neck
& forced to make a scar exhibit
marched round the social marketplace
with thoughts tied, stock phrases   foul-mew
     seagoing   outspeak of a dying
generation deposited on the attention menu
under unfamiliar sole
         screeds of gorgeous stars
while the world of high-frequency
trading turns over delicately   weaponry & fear
and what's outside
         revelation, past betrayal
is this I'll need to stammer after waking.
The children we'll never have
         whisper to me in wall-shadows
to send them a life
     stings what's visible   lunar
iris blur, tap on the empty tin
lap of the eaten evening light
         welt words go spraining into that dark.
I felt genuinely screwed   terrified
     you'd learnt to hate me
what we'd tried to whip up crumbling
         into retaliation & self-retaliation
seeding deeply, projected away   taken as truth.
One of those raw weeks
where suicide seems like the only
     art possible in a mercenary time

when the permanews is engineered crisis
and at the cellular level
anxiety & shivering   wars no fucker wanted
except a vulture pressure driven wild by numbers
                          by its own delirious transfer
every poem robbed back
          from compelled speech
birdsong the bolt in perpetual   plated nightmares
who I'm talking to's nothing
                weeds & scraps in the street.

What we make, reverberating
gathered together
                alters things
sometimes only in the littlest way, for
the most insignificant
                spore of time you can imagine
but in strange weathervane veering   wrecks
& jolts, not the sentimental heart shift
       but a penumbra way clear of naming,
                       devouring, discipline
stepping off through the snowy portal
               not leaving anyone behind
dead or disappearing
          unseen or unborn
among failed nations, prisons   the cremated meadow
keystone coral, lung
          bleach & moth scales
               raining from greed.
Space yawns its pointless
desire, whatever   the rich
     have their cubicles. A financial district
full of reasonable team players
           passed by pissed
                 is shatterable glass
a common bandage, I'd mother
          the dogshit & tree stumps
to keep me from shutting down
            when the dreaming clears
      and the bloom ripcords
most alright people   nearly spent
but fixed to frames & beams & one another
          fastened to the starry
                rush in the branches.
Public pepper, private steel, public order

    this spoke from pyroclastic daybreak
                    I'm just coughing at the junction
unabsolved, blown apart
          murmuring to someone new
                                  a scratch on the air

PATENT

coarse stars   and the tongue sea
destined to persuade

peep paving rills.   skim unsure
      where I'm headed
in a near nest mow dream

the lithium mine

that lyric chrysalises
would not be co-bowed to

fracture of a past mouth, duress-spinney
fire & fire   up to the shutter.

another nocturne, one for the season   in a void of gulls
slice of the boundary
dandelion gleam
          field steeple
of unkilled
imagination
                reeling on arrival

and it will never bring you peace

                but it plummets from the rafters

there in a wave and a light

RUFFORD PARK POACHERS

    the water lily is   above your lease
        sky unwinds incurable
            illegible   as this place
place is talons
          a stone or counter-shell
        disgraces no one
goshawk talkative   falling
        into the fireside
                          when fired kindness
breaks in me
              all tracks
        all narrow call   lives
                are what we lux-look for

SONG: LUNG BUD

    step inhumanly over the pavement
    no luck my superior
        I'm off now
                broke wish sparring

    clutch of big tunes
    rush the publicists of our time
        quick to a synapse
                hand in the trap

MARKET PSYCHOLOGY

Anubis the jackal.   flashing halter on a fined sea-sky
that dawning of senselessness & vicious peace you wake to
we get cloaked in it
there is carnivorous specialism edging towards you now
    across the custom city.   fuck composure. O windlass
I have written myself into a shadow of enumerated life.
the insanity of our poetry. that is not to be broken open
that is the by-product of bridling phobias, spheres needles
        rubber bullets chaotic doubt
wasting all the binding shit I've muttered this far in my worthless life
our writing met with silence
            our names on the receipt.

what else is there to lose.
think for a second of any stream trinket not the corporate-state algorithm
dictates how the bloodstained social stockpiles
lives into accounts
which may be targeted engineered and eaten whole.
what would it mean to get up one day and say to yourself
& your missing friends & the sound of roadworks
rising from the street below
that you will not be eaten whole.
not newsworthy. I'm keying this in full of faraway fire
most supermarket things you do are unopened parachutes
            a person was killed.
too many slid off from here. each one governed. peaceably.
picowave   lag pied wagtail
mizzle thoughts in bits again
groggy to a flogged history clawed at
not allowed to you or really any of us
noise of it grating on outlet souls
when the language of true north
        earths.

because I hate this shithole archipelago, hate the only ruined music
I can make through my bad teeth
show us how to pass undamaged
weather torus   rabbit gather   little tinny
bossing it keeping the wards at bay

obedient journalists spokespeople would harass you, you
should never encroach on their career territory
or listen to middle class heartlessness
are basically the Home Office. drip decade of being remedied
remedied & laughed on by posturing bronzes
their desirable moral economy showy renunciations of harm
    but you must stick up for your tarpit
everyone acting like line managers
I'm lighting this wrong I'm June on the quick
flower of no going place
dilly-dally runoff shift
     wick slash in the shooting dark
when wage labour splits your nap hayloft
there where I am barely even hilly any longer
poem the only thing chime-coating me
the 'community' removes wasters & junkies
on this ladder you gob on whatever's lower than you
that's human nature
Rigel mangy towering fumes
may the scroungers rise through the park

now memorise this flyer
and then pour hydrochloric acid over it until it completely dissolves
turn into the low green glow
hum & rustle clough & aster
slanting on towards our nattering
Scald Law's lippy star
equipping me with sticky weed & lapis lazuli
when death is riding through the night
but we won't go with him
art has been this porous earthwork
braced against a life's catastrophe
I hold it in my head, I hold your head in mine
    and we are the telluric ones

THERMAL STORAGE

Getting it down over a quack November night, the 16th
shroud cold   at the tail-end of a year
when I almost forgot what poetry is, why it's done, why indigo tongue
         or bolstered lash, ignoring how we lock off

no matter if that's dissonant   ripped
Google wish
to lie detector, I let it happen to me
         gone for a living

two pliable lungs   won't weaken
but suddenly so clear & calm
and Tom they're not having my attention
         the way we unmoored
wood dip cashing, thinking these sheets could be shook fire
the city the scratch coat the less detectable
if to mention options   is shop chat
sleeping body on the corner, early warning spray
         in darkness
that employee pain
         could wipe itself out

what props up the desperate world   brink lance
each sure spark   under the boot
under the moon
canal bolt-blue, changing states with substance data
I'd be believed
or bleeding from the corner of the mouth   a dayful returns
so always   on the edge of being defaced

my only duration, my
sling-summer scale,
my finite
trace

GIVING BACK

an arrangement that modernises us into passive dogs

broadcast hourglass
task mutt in lunar squalor

had to sit with a man who owns his own company
discussing his watch
beau of my beau, clone of the sheen

appears now in front of our tired eyes like an oceanic tong
the only trend is the mutation of what is

THE SERVANT AND THE STICK

painkillers. a revenue cloud. green foyer
      under the donors into the forest, to feel accursed

the country I was born in to die in
          to know a fledgling on the end of a rope

    collectivism the spot in the ointment
            means win your gas & electricity bills paid for a year
give the wheel a proper spin phil

      'a mound of rubbish like that
is bad for business. we did not undermine the strike'

            scurf scarper into the firth sewer
I'm a peasant moon
    blow me south, lord. lord, pin me into the larder

               that's what I really need to want
a mountain of student apartments small plates manor psalms
      all gentleness pretence, everything taken away

              the benevolent stoop the window assassinated
sight of tearing national eagles out of tall lawns & second homes

      O my life would be pointless
           if I couldn't serrate myself

CASTOR AND POLLUX

> I shall
>   with doubt
>   bloom in my season
> —Stephen Jonas

I

It was a dream of writing. News grazed the world, fires
tangled with clouds, the wreckage of the social
in the last calendar year
Amazon posted a net revenue of $386bn.
But let this find
        a loosening in my chest.
Waiting for the virus to fucking eat me
how is it possible
Wraith jargon, reopening
I cast back to the first shawl months of our unhappiness | fraudster traffic
in the cities of grey sorrow & insomnia
the Right in universal power, heir & heiress art
    on every link & channel. Three decades of
a sick hearts airports
hearing the music of property development, bitter
arraignment, the less lethal air. 13 minutes
since I started doing this. Sloganeering~ vacancies~ respawn
Our songs burst forever
Flower & fence
Sparrow distress call
        from the pavement fucks me up instantly
pausing on another Gigafactory, Mace Group
summons west of gorgon zone. | Swine whites~ heat loss
Have we ever been alive. Time
demands a sort of sworn intention, *work–life balance*
        Thousands of ways to hawk your soul
Sometimes I feel incomprehensible
like my whole minds gone to the dogs. Or we're wrapped
in banner ads, latching on non-native
larch, fume-tagged, butchered, Penguin Random House
    A tech stare examines the Strait of Dover.

II

Give up. Work yourself to death.
How did the earlier poets hold it together. Incinerating
ecotours~ storm turn~ salt barb
            Redrow plc portfolio. Everyone's a cynic some days
in this valley of adders where all things are bought & sold
it is not for nothing
sky imperfect | diesel-rainbow
       July's hare in a surge
Knowing ingrown toxins, the condescension of cultural institutions
as I finish this dishonest cover letter to management
                               drags the heart out of me.
To envisage other paths of actually being here
immortals are nearby, light
pelts us expensively, surgical, the dragon light.
           What was 'humanity'. Lilac shadows
Only a nauseating idea
assault weapons flags hung over the fields & the brunt of the sea
embers of Hölderlin, infinite Uber
Pemex on the surface of the Gulf of Mexico
      or flying in these shelves of cancerous smog.
Makes me almost forget who I am.
To somehow crawl on our knees through the refining fire.
A ruined commitment, not
maturity, or fate, or quietism, or any of that bollocks they question
you about, still a commitment
climbing slant roads in the rough reach of an afternoon
not misused
                          wren-worlds billowing
What wit mutilates around a barycentre~
Interview panels of professional leftists.
I'd be lying if I made out I could see into the future
from the kitchen table draining my drink
         A bolt gun hymn
thinking quietly up Nicky Nook
or stepping lost through a familiar city without a name
That polite manipulators with enough money in the family
were rewarded with careers, estates, 'unpaid internships' | starred
              & striped ascension
while the rest rotted or burned out or were hospitalised.
What can I send you to take away into the earth.
Posted tokens
soundbites the cutlass means to platform renown

        social cleansing of Manchester by corporate interests
because they were taught nothing else, nothing else was allowed
(I found a pied wagtail and it spoke to me)
But the battered class and the sucked shortfall of that history
attrition~ pay freeze~ creeping juridical innocence
intertwined with the Tesla ecosystem
        won't ever be devoured or destroyed. Not completely.
Love of poetry, friends & visitors echoing
through windtorn towns & residential areas
where they slow to ground. A culture that created anti-homeless spikes
Gaunt sun spools like the root of theft
        trading packages of toxic debt
Terrified I'll never write a thing again. This hurt cleaves past.

III

No freedom for the barely living
in & out of breath. The park was amazing last night until skies
        went atrocious, gutted, stillborn, last-ditch
thoughts of getting wrecked, realms of abusive shit & dust.
What do any of us mean.
Jut tongue~ Deutsche Bank~ Viable on impact
        I plague you so, so much
And this is not a promise to be alright with it or good
but to keep mangling the normal truth
about the governments & market leaders of the world, ruthless
-ness & blood. | You know some cords a poets lot is morbid frailty
a window horizontal over water
Evening lunges in. I'm frightened &
exhausted by the thought of everything there is to lose,
        everything already lost or crushed
stars bind Colonsay
stay along me or it's done. Now
I've found the burn once more, though my noise is breaking
my words ripped to shreds. What else is this cruel.
The poet will never die
        and they'll move gracefully forever
in the errant places that they made, fabric of ultramarine
cantilevers greening in the lift
stray arches of our swerve purpose
A threshold to hang on to
down the blowing years out in front. Hydrangeas in streetlight.
        My song is on the planets. It will not be for nothing

SONG: MIRE DRUM

raked by silences
        language rides a thaw thought

the spore in the lash
        where you dismember lies

conceals what town mechanisms
        spin us into reef spur radiance

                still straying, uncaptured

COCKATRICES AND ECHOES

Postures not hunted
less needed, it dell-dawned
       all slain shuddering summer
better off alive
like blazes
that this too was what they named 'the west'
under an ice slug sky~
the palace in which
our sports have an end
decree kill one
another
then lie   marram grass & still future.

Still laugh. The pinpoint
struck by town clockfaces
moves knotweed, not
ever to reflect a wintry stronghold where a soloist could rage
(*Long live the squires*)
        lobbed unpredictably to bullseyehood

but innocence is a cloak~
gateau clouds ate & known

Bitterless
undowned north hares by the kerb

HUMAN FACTORS

that there are gaps, crevices
to escape through. pass signals. but that the cage is as real
as any night ballad, night sky
spreading like black mould over the adjourned horizon

and that this move would mean dismemberment
hidden in packaging, a hand, an ear
you build fissures

like a lost mammal relates to its own amputation
kissing in an ancient poem
or a grey hill's forehead
or your first day of primary school

the only way to be spared
is to follow brutish instincts
a little algorithm told me
and so morning arrives with its sterile consequences

learn to hunt. die in poverty. decimate
the opaque life that trembles between buildings, the
abyss in the core
lie of a person, lording it over some basic shard

right now it makes
a sort of halfsense to carve
wards on fragile innermost amulets
against hardening storms

so that we have the strength
to interrupt, follow trails to capsizing,
glamorous twinge of the light up there

Dom, sack it off for today
creak of woodpeckers

STATE FUNERAL

well now I think I get what it's like to be ashamed
and we never really knew our mums & dads, and the rain scale
ratcheting up on the pentlands
shunt spill off, is like a pigsty dream

the queen will finally be dead soon
then the people who killed themselves will walk out of the sea
and a country will burn away

not bending the knee like a true citizen, admiring
dead coral, psychotic laws, the
king james bible.
you can't tell the water what to do
however much you want to

wait on the table or lacerate the daystar
a lifetime of service

and maybe the poets are still scheming in the clouds & pits

wishbone to larynx
through pines, hazels. sunken perception.
all that's left of us
choke turned

a pauper's grave
becomes a palisade

all that's left in this slight room
the sunflowers whorl brought
when you didn't get another job & said
you didn't want to be here anymore

voices. what you throw
tune town. the lurch in the a.m.

PLAQUE'S HEAP

> Facing three ways,
> Welcoming wayfarers
> —H.D.

> And to brave clearness all things are reduc'd.
> —John Donne

Mite time's leaked twilight
imagines a beaker with a
             glaive through it...

Puck's leap
to never lay low in nickel, under bouncing cloud cover
preserve of my infra ant injury

The phones are voids. Then we'll leave them

     lustrous at dock
bottom   just a poem plunges across
fire & water, chancy
I'm really where I
am in this sane mode of sheep scab

         Clown's northerly stellar aisle

    dials terrains of
chlorine soil on Bourne Hill, so blue, then red, saving the fleet football
scatterjacks over a pleated chorography
ex-skyscrapers
candidate pigshit

Jettisoned to
vital discomfort   that now I guess
I do squintly stand under

      It doesn't cut us off from lily lives
small against formless rocks

        it knows mind & art exit the function room~

dare deep & depart the green glen

to hurl a wet exoskeleton at
                lagging machine cogs

& let a fable balloon
                      float up
above the planetary woods

This is inexactness & cuticle
        courage, huge, torn thicket, not to get where things go

zipping out of the
park minus my felt bag, sheer biosphere
mazed   halfdreaming the hoopoe

Hi teal towpath
                draped with a studding-star blanket, snus
Lost your nan's quartz   the checkout world sendoff
lunglike supernatural remembering

Hi ancient friends & dusty rigging sky

Spit in the eye or don't spit in the eye

At diving dawn
the Hillhouse scop drops
& rolls around in a
ripply mac   trials rainbow forestial

(air-lens
       trading penknives
oracling)

                      Ta ra to sharp shales

for the aftermaths unfracked   but waving
to abandon killing prop~ floored comeback stylite

and wide weal work to do
                      beyond.

I can see the stragglers glowing in the stolen earth
        and take his paw. It's quiet.

A slow life to sew

Burr on burr and harsh
                swimming down the hurlyburly

With this grass touch
I clap a lovely topyard welter
in our unmended

harping headache   Do I?
        Cloakroom word loud. At all. No thought banished.

LUG POEM

slip leaf blower
down edge of slip city, sound, down to where sound shins
and hedge tune tows me
so I'm no one in the poem

lotus tugboat
declaratives go and dissolve, in time, shut lark, what you think
stutter beyond militarism
NATO fractals
a high trait skips

but lucky as nothing in sounds
your ones, link mine as loot
tip syrinx

that there'd be styles of future, lag
riverbank
crates, rayon
belonging somewhere
it matters, nova from peony, slacking

the poem's what we do together
not just dead shit we're inside, not only this, tearing creates
pink birdair, wild mauve early over
low houses, the enclosures, chirrup & hiccup &

off out for a dance

VISUAL SNOW

hard to write a draught excluder, hard to stop
to pick up half a vocal cord from the drain
and call it love, therell be frameworks
there will be flavourless stoic watchtowers
dotting the manufacture of knowledge
that outside the last bar or the upswing of the bus
as it catches my sheer hollowness in the street
a collision of these things
with urgency of all others, smiling for once
with the need to make tiny sounds & mess
like a bird from a big vented column of natural gas
singes away, a whelk outdoors
in the scarred heart of occupying evidence
there was no halt to any of this, you know it
the point was surrender
that passes surrender

WAR BLUR

We swam to a source but it was no source

Cassiopeia over
far ovals from pine resin~
        bright letter in a belt boy's handwriting

That's your feather & urn
                ribo, peered at, latch-late
to the beheading game

The woods not ours or hell's
elder from older from alder

and heard obelisks in the after
blinded,
kindred
spoil trefoil bots in you

spoil disciplining chickens
      that own the springs

Hummingbird's heart when I was like 19
stoned by the weir wild hunt
Star trusting noone
black bib in a sun
bush to mow me
         now

translating
lie toxin, unruppelled, tannin

When with bitter money
submarines
make over
your visor
into frackable scarecrows for
      murder use

blow up the projector

dive light
your
laning organs

eight chalices
left to script speech
yours & type in anti-delve

hunker
under tiltrotors

The old shame tor
          by cave world
is a detained thought
turned iris

Aisle language siloed, and words
      are chime children
poets lose track of in the night

for blea's utmost counter

never may become the spit
of fake assailants~ their
                    understanding

vended, climbing, path spore

Lonely lean-tos
and future fathoms

Half of that hummingbird
rebels in nectar

UNNUMBED

the back of the head
is a clear clock
turning away. the star hits my
cup
and sinks
as a scurry tone

it's your poem
put some spin on it
writing towards dander
through traumata
racket
of the hired city, these
least lesions
the good incompetence
whisht the pretense

I know my rabbit life
is a collision taunt
do you?
beacons fly beelining
only way taken
by scruff from
maestros & masters
'a world against friendship'

that fort's
demo shreds, decent ~ landscape-carry in tote
while two heartsease
scent, stroke my bedhead when I walk
and all is halfway fucked & fine

ee how girder bird
bits site
reverse-maim.
no rescue ~ a syntax to ring off
yoyoing Pluto
cricks livery

equal mix
the lant canal, a heapword
held me
to beautiful darkness, it did so

this little place specific
table, salt pot
horizons-ladder-of
it did so
first line of one, a blue met chance
eleventh day

HERNE THE HUNTER

wasn't that l'histoire catamaran
      spewed inevitably me

into contact with teal
          loitering voices

                chance a tool heat death uses

     the living room's spiked angle
from a mind of homicides

    swaddling salvo

        where it's real to exhale

sometimes life doesn't go on.   normal world

          to head out every day past
    machines that can break you if they want to

in the name of speed, stat

a poem about how I'm a nice person.
                             a poem high as the last hide
     evicted by developers

unplace wild sea thrift (knows pinkish)

                blinks   shoo
  the war broadcast.

today colour
    is the attempt

                        propeller mush

     noise paint

our ugliness, like a turned tarn splitting

                              quidrack horizon

spring still desired us, it moves. viola
            from the cascading window palms you away
      to a plication

                  resurrects wewill   weapon trichord

strangers with mental illness don't deserve housing

      the night grabbed by conscious wrecktype.

                                    but each other
customer left hours ago
            and the rag moon is up

    reforming the life-support
out of a deep dream

            it never works.

like at the end of the film   wally shawn
                        through the starred cab
      floats back to a blanket

                  not so much or
                                    changed

to heel hover at the terminus
            I'll need some of me left

bracing to several

      steel weather we
      can't steer

                              as the lordly city, weakened
      grass under my shoes

a poet abolishes himself

            a poet does not abolish himself

HYMN FROM CAREERS

Noise invades

meadow foxtail

Archways of conceptual stomach

the law of the clan

Purchase power

gasp rifting from

Get the tune in your sights

branching of bustle snot

go a fit on my bill

cloud tunic tump

duck wisdom in what a pal tells us

rails at us in starts

doc leaf

the raising of the coffin

tin on skin egg

Double-helix space in

my two-faced form

inherited language

a cheese at fourpence, bovine

There's no good time to write

price of dying

what was a shield, court poetry

trance & a daw cap through a dust storm

squatting in cynical off-climate

to absolutely bottle it

Novichok tree creep

wrap the snub in your mantra

a vessel of narcissists

ledge music

battery, to have come back round

in what assailant speak

porch light

rain anvil

mash on bourbon

lake on stapler

urgency of pond matter

Tear up your death certificates

stood there like

in the act of altering a sense of living time

parliament scent in tongues

this burst of inscribing

fellow shovelers

need to find which way to look

Braid Burn

vertical sun hoard

chained to Bank of Scotland blot

what sold the driveway

Real terms in laps

or airport spook expanding

to pass the razor back

the street between my teeth

not paid on mass

ebb of firth is a cur movement

nuclear war

bluffs that grew up rich

rib the gripe totally

As for us glugs

but open Grace

they say that you just have to not belt up

nonsense racket

pissing about on the links

seconds turn

                          This one out of the hat

                              meat core bussed

                      I forget the wrong order

                      thumb sound to hang from

                mural pay for trust fund wank

                          or a wasp on a crust

                          who owns the water

when old Tom got up one day behind your flat

                                  bashed by HS2

                                One big poem

hit of geography as spontaneous combustion

                    and gas cut off or threat

                            shepstare runaway

                    when they're talking about

                        Students of marketing

                                only compete

                    typed out, concrete's thick

                          wheelspin for months

                                Muriel or Baz

                    through killing blankness

                  I am my sibling's peat wit

                    our syntax in arson babble

                                           missing people
sawtooth going up at every edge & rim
                                           we don't skimp on
concentration of shanks
                                           crude forecast in 'medium-term'
too screentired to think most nights
                                           it's what they want
keep you in your place nodding
                                           luxury airway
Thiel bunker
                                           to waste away in counting
when shit hits the fan
                                           an unwired panic button, weird calls
off Switzerland & France
                                           you've not fell yet
Agility was my maiden name
                                           the metaverse is a birdcage
bot in the income diptych
                                           but spring spits its crocus behind my ear
in honour of ancient grease
                                           fields burn through my head
yellow-legged
                                           skyscrape yell
left behind to destroy docks
                                           This is a text on the vampire jubilee
half-chewed by Human Resources
                                           gorse flicker
flecked blacklist
                                           about to bat the Milky Way
stinger on a rack rush
                                           We've been at war with the grave
who's been in the shrug basement
                                           in thrall to assassin spires
So one trainer in front of the other
                                           a curious phantom forages me
that all of this is worth our names
                                           from scunnering June spindrift
grief ding of lovers
                                           every fucker in the purl
cuffs & rags bow to a despair cult
                                           hanging on that bench by wrecked rood abbey
scent hound bombing
                                           the royal leech
drill through planks
                                           public trepan for replies

that what I hate

and chips away

exists inside gut lawns

crawlspace of the poem

wheatgrass for my bracelet

to enclose & measure art & thought

found in BAE Systems

I almost went to love

then dynamo resistance

cook the leashes

when a thousand dumb

get us at the bar before

now make the cymbal here

is what recycles me

A barm in the block's shared garden

furnace empire

tack lashed the underfoot

Pioneering academic fields

must not bestow

sergeant ethics of the orbiting class

my own stock unhappiness

meet with a printer

failed for words when one phone froze

resentments crumble

You sent me Eastman's *Femenine*

weather in squares

THREE

CRUDE THOUGHTS

I'll leave, but loudly   I'll leave
my heart will never be broken.
the city lobotomy. skin crawl. all written wrynecks said bits
crowd back onto me   jinx
            early lyre by sheaf shops
night through noon at once
flow gentle sauteing of
the frontal cortex. the final human songs
                  recline me in this accelerating garden
first words to scrim the dawn
fracture & stow
did parents colleagues hurt you
do you use a mashed sentence
as an envelope   of weal-world
your yellowhammer
            yellowhammer's you, you
under sickle moon flitting
shape   or just an eight-foot masque
camouflage steals my soul
                        into the lead twilitness.
seen 'crafts of nonhuman origin'
but trusted the notepier
            fruiting out an ouzel gorge
that tells us anything we want   sweet Afton
poetry arc line holding at bay stuff pain
            tries to get you to do.
elusion was mythic   plane on a brass cloud
wifi misdirect
stepped-on pomegranate venom in a film. this kind. seen
Skippool creek burned down
      by the redshanks   boat cemetery
funged in phantom havoc
            loop wing matinee
I'm not one with my hide.
hatred bleat   pig pivot. copyright. the victors word
misnamed the inside for the out
brung clad-capering funerals
to an altar where the wind on Russian grass
      in the mirror surpasses a refractory figure

social impact of my art
minused from the equation.
                          replaced by robots.
O rival poacher, my speech therapist
               youve learned zilch, but everything I couldn't, can't
prohibition music   music of ability
mirrorgullet diverging
to survive,   mirror gull
trashed with a talon in your kidney.
      but we were hopeless & alive.
                         and we were summer-poisoned.

the hypnotists inherit the sea. the sea
inherits my merry mind.
cocoon sellers, still kicking about, still
              icy to touch with the bare pad.
just me   I think soon as you nail down a *poetics*
too rigid you trap yourself ferroconcrete.
      theres enough sundews in the setup and
we never were pure.
horizon pissed with dragonflies
nettle in my buttonhole
who says
karaoke is shit   the mad are real
        only under the microscope
and each emotion
you know big as a razor comet.
yesterday John Keats tripped down a little branch
           to see me, John Keats when I wouldnt sleep
and Pudding the cat.
too gouged by dominion to help, scissors
converging in the dream of a split personality
              I sound violent, pity from heaven
pitterpatters lie joust. the
heiling praise of aesthetics
alone. impossible   to support shadows
who can't look after ourself fade me into
the deepest thicket of light. sanity governs
two-channel   like you mean
      outrage on schedule.
                          extravagant skyfolds.
paint me as one of your midsummer mornings
in the carbon days after 7/7
so that I bibe singlethought but each nearby is calving in
      prose   thats not my well manner

yelled things
sent honey towards Carlisle
      wired pollen to Chapeltown
troubadour disorganises
    fumelands, knights, passes
muster. so I'll be the waylayer
built of lunacy   wont waste free thieved minutes
making lang objects that sound dead
as the blood-glacier producing us
   tin of mackerel   may my voice
move differently than that, it moves differently
it ruins art
art no menhir but
    boreal summons from the individual 'genius'
invested in legal pesticide, prosecution
whicker   talk of justice
brought low by corrupt files /
airconditioned pavement /
sun on the cliffs
    the perfect
      militarised revenge.

and also lathe of love, Eurydice & the daisy stars.
gratitude, not to maestros
    but to the cobugs. which is a game of
pingpong. look high enough for swallow
-altereds I lost our
listlessness. memories
of enemies, just memories, beer yard willow.
no dice. the rupture of a trance
tiptoeing towards grace in the background of the metropolis
   a full quiver   I can hardly write
this. we eat one another by force
we have bad posture through the forest of Pendle.
breath gauze from a fire   hollow skyscrapers
  become the true vision of Valhalla they
always shot for
take the place of a
fell, retire to the chalet & live off crab apples drown my phone
    chew the cud. the world of
love that isnt a world. the
world that canters away to Lavenham. fuckyeah
wild rotation
the flammable word. mutiny, an iris
      on the shores of crystal orphanhood

A SALAMANDER

Now poems feel
majorly gnawed
problems this immortal second~ rubied
half-days

some battered continuing subtalk
        and you've got to sow wheat in the welkin

I walk down any high street.
The teeth on the news are a riddle.
Anchovy earth~ Sort code gob

For my next trick
treble clefs, branchings

THE END OF MELANCHOLIA

blood and tonic, whiplash dashing
                               like an earth sprite

swaying ahead of Neptune
mined unstable ices   sleeper blues

           to surrender cruise control
swift host honing to the lovers

dove bulwarks waking in deforested night

    so that my scant dialect resolves
whats multigenerational

its baited death   then claw-sediments
                               psychic history

into dear reefs of farm
animals freed

             a suppler tone and tragic carpet
angel cutlery brokered into kerosene

                    blows art prose

the season that stays yours
when agilitys
       perfect business

             curl curtain over bluebell level
our curfew

hyper song-perk hiking in
             pain sites

I have a burnt   ladder in my eyes
so a breach in my head.

a poet who language happened to

(deftness thanks
the tide　　　　　　that chews grains out your palm)

who got buffeted, hunting

for a chafing
stance

　　　　　　so that
sheens fell away, your shinsplints

in Formia　　　　　　　your
overdue feet

still morning rose up with one barred blackbird in its throat.

will you have me home. which is
　　　　　　　　　　　　　　nowhere but
this, the barn licks back
robed freon

and grief is a light motor. stolen by neglect

by shit lives of rejection and recrimination
　　　　　　　　　　works that vastly amortised over mouths

from double sickness
　　　　　　the flag of furnaces turned forward

which I hold to my veering iceberg

as if I'm　　　　　a testable
　　　pipistrelle
with no sworn place to dip

　　　　　　　　　　thorn justice as the opening principle

here is a rag of holes
　　　　　　here is the sorrow to carry

here are the mad and ignored

　　　　　　　　　　here is your wince-glass of music
abolishing proud silent judges

                fenced Parnassus kicked out to nothing

    what can you hear in the hazel?
                                        a dream will belong to itself

MUCK FOR MAY DAY

gamut-wings
between graves & fronts
my life is a standing scarp or
a piano that becomes a deed.

baron chlorophyll fills our heads
with woody laws
malodorant then canvas history

the moon & stars like beetroot, turnips
kiss a rebellion a bright strand
slain in the work of middleclass fiends
this cant be a balm. grievous grand. hands off

the workhouse swims in   I
wrote blooded songs because I wanted to be loved
affirm cosmic sorrel flowers I loved

warred May
the next words mean little but grazes
my commitment was to love & beauty.
I remember when I'm reedless in the alley.

WATER AND ARMOUR

> there, beyond the borders of day, the insurrection has begun
> —Galina Rymbu

a torrent skip to talk on sleek
        songheels
aubergine overturns in the Milky Way

        found anfractuous
route back to poems
each one's like beginning all over again from the harp ending

first speech   language snows
lovely into a stranger's lap

the hugest offence you can imagine to artificial scarcity
                      spreadsheet life
unsound as a fake pound coin

but I worry that optimism shreds, offscourings
are like bourgeois litter

        then glue-grasp the isolating inner   & planetary despair
can't be allowed to decimate us
    12,000 unique hues of red cloud

this ocean-change, spoken.

I've not often written calmly
        Wharf shuffle in lone lank leaf

difficult to in a belt of fires
        requiem at my ear was a nautilus

dancing like no one's arsed.

    a corner you'll never stop turning   infinite copper downpour
and new education by mucking in

you with gardeners in Pollokshields
sunslang, deadheaded
     giving a toss every day

not to be seen too often, not for the admiration of electrified fences
what hostility fragments us

        banning trade unions
  torque sooth   still fentanyl

I don't think utopia actually has a name.
a careful house, reeds   a reckless one

    healable talon

that lad getting his number taken
       wick of the wind through rift canopies
  sleet wing sailing
      siren blackbirds

when nothing makes any sense to me
not whisper song

where grief is a skerry.   and our art,
    absolutely broken, burned at low tide.

so bad at telling what I feel & think
berg-numb, trapped   unable to mourn the lost
    in systemic memento mori
  I turn to the mess of my poems.

communism a bow & arrow
we each could carry

a gift from the woods of the dead.

the beam at my back   rung plume for a foot
a wave round my knuckle
     deep in July.

your work says
sky-chore weaves on   allay.

and what else really now is there to be
       a flaw eating hearts

        through wrong sharp chaos of this unlife

                but affirm that other daylight
disfiguring the lot

                      is here already   in the smallest acts

ODE TO SPIT

The world will come after you
              flame blow goldcrests casting about
                            sunburnt sill & the gasp of roads
                                        in steep churned burgundy light
slashed from a proper racket, counterfurling.
              My lung talk runs ragged then gorgeous
                            landing on a form was a principle
                                      mortality & money followed.
At different tilts of the poem
              I stand in front of you slyly or the Irish Sea
                            thinking meat, powerful buildings far away
                                    tusk cuts shan through my chest
and are we in chunks now. Or restored. Or a cog in the dilemma.
              New mutation ground up, glow grip
                            how many senses turn against you
                                    acid sleet hinting at private deals
the smell of a starved town
              Say the whole sun is theirs, out of fuel
                            ask what more can figurines take
                                    Blackout track done to hell.
But I would sweep myself under this place.
              We want it as a style of lightning
                            though must pass most of our time working or asleep
                                    a corner of the outrageous system
Balkanised, it doesn't have to cohere if it's moving.
              Debt traps in the air, state secrets daydreaming outside
                            I ventilate this hopeless house
                                    and it becomes a rose of rain
tougher to drown the mind's own statues
              in our dreck condition
                            poets evaluating each other
                                    acquired by an agent or flag
fitting together their asphodels, discussing 'extremism'
              tied up in boutique obsolescence
                            having submitted it all.
                            Then we suss bad blight out, omen wand

       antenna found antenna
                what flavour is the rangy sky
                         remixing while Wyre floods
                                while Leith dies of boring hipsters
sipping batch brew
        a sort of unlicensed spark
                constitutional monarchy like a set of vices
                        hand in hand with my heart
and never crossing over to the Isle of Man.
        Katy, I think I forgot how to swerve for a bit
                skull opened to the elements by Surgeons' Hall
                        now fire curls on our shoulders
under a rosewood cloud
        or fuchsia unslaked waves
                engulfed in the maw of the faulty Zukunft
                        so send me your promontory or pier
remind me that what's fucked is fully living
        the dead in that satellite nearest the planet
                merciless employers
                        Goya's dog
quicksand, shade
        as I stumble off into the bare balked fells.
                Or tell yourself it's only an illusion
                        dupe music & limitless starling murmur
we are alive in the terrible global village together
        unlearned to factory settings
                glimpsed through sea frets
                        and dear damage, haggard space
a fieldfare flares in the font of numbers
        botching the last apocalypse before you know what's happened
                bugs that veer in the night
                        haven't sweated so much in weeks
Smack the thermostat. Art is along conveyance, until it stutters
        song's fluorescing obscurities
                the grain of hidden objects
                        slant presence & whipstall
it freed a cuticle or a few notes
        it bled us dry
                threw me on a javelin path
                        worth more than all the trillions
banked in the airbrushed fucking earth
        And if we waste it, that's alright.
                In torn time you'll go wherever you need
                        without possession or papers

see it through or end in the job.
            A jongleur is never not mauled
                      by bevvied nightmares
                                  Neuralink tightening like a garotte
I leave this here
        in a wild chance so we can find one another.
                      Even if shit gets broken off us
                                if next year I'm an abraded silhouette
rat on who I used to be, or might be.
            Amnesiacs traded down the tributary for magic beans
                    the going rate's shut reverie, dire day
                              desperate for old wisdom
give me my scallop shell of bloody murder
            the twilight is beautiful too
                    petals marking the expanse
                              in advance of everything.
Luke, this is the strapped edge of the sky.
            A nation of bastards. What can we do to our lives
                    what figure or shape would work as the flint
                          of song itself
through the happiness of leeches & snakes
            and mega-rich nihilism arrayed against our ferns.
                    Anyone's lectern implodes.
                          I am writing this almost losing it
at the crossroads of what's in me to transmit
            no argument to nick in disbarred dreams
                    'but there's plenty on the dole
                          in the land o' the leal'
And though the backlash slams into us like a taxi
            I trust what beaks scar
                    skew the scenery and flee the scene
                                in tamped turmoil of this airspace

I LOVE TO WALK THE FIELDS

an animal wrote this. the blue debtor
    delphiniums didnt neglect
                  us or the rainedon covert
or the stet stereo wood dial

this all shorn   morn up I listened to endangered noise.

dell weft waiting to growover separating wire
            selfcare to sell you shit
compiled in blood tomes, histories of english poetry
    a calm old handkerchief waving at my other face

to really get it, inhabiting repudiation from wall-figures
    when all you brought, trying, was numbered
        unmet   by moon miles.

I set else to make amazing art with anyone I saw
            back them to find the poems they could
because it swayed days dazzling
    not rip them down, shunned, sent away ashamed

like the pathetic words & deeds of
    mainlanders who live the propaganda, only to multiply money
        furnish private booths & lockers of ersatz happiness
reinforced by empire-emptiness, cavorting over whoever the news says is lesser

    art that created realities, brought down
        governments, 'worked for the birds'.
            will want it til I head & past that bend.

but you can't be battered out of dolour, the conquered
outside psypsy-battle, unwashed, I thank
    you for holding me to suppleness & the kindquestioning that
transmutes. always so   much wilder than judges.

      matted acts of braveness, the awkward
          take on the nightclub newly fed. end to
duty, bad bardic silence, stone paeans
              close of screening~

'moral purity' (its scarecrow too) coerces itself into a lethe corner
while the richest people you
 know tell each other off forever in a vacuum that they own.

 syrinx unadjudicates I sheer shed so much
erotics of soil & rosehip. first poems.

you could slash & type &
chirr so strawly strange that strangle-bots will
 never learn or replicate it tock tock.
yaw & throw off the snare camera heaven
 needing momentary
seclusion, hiding clefs, then to step togetherawe

 no more castigating constellated self or sud.
clumsy poem as its own made reader hurried out
hurt leap to lushly
playing the keyboard
 never to succumb

AUREOLE

that I stick on my hat down a slow street
where the westronwind
catches us totally
off guard ~ distal greenfinch ~ goldenrod   in lieu
of opal ornaments, loving the ground & loving acted October light
on a spiderpoem that plant-links
              a lot fortuitous, bluely, faraway

singers undersharing a stony heart
opened by goats in Chagall
you build the house at the turning of time
the house builds our own day
                      every devil lived, intensifying
and death makes a dancer cully
my leap life's flying through tunes that started things

gossamer minds old spunout
summer to slum it, truly, Lyra leaves in the cityflow & nightshade
descriptions dithers done
so gone world tells you you're too much for it
      serry songs of our creating
I've no holt, patch the sauce for a year
beach towns write this down about history

bird murmur, from damage chord
that cares less ~   'working on my joy
i experienced autumn', and youyou
slant with an animal, as an animal
                      one who lets twin halos rust moonsun-rightly
the passionatest rat in Orion   insolent out the rows
give music us to fellflower

is a grimy feathered little 'lad', ay
out-earthed by what the holders spoke a 'lass'
I step off the dawn cliff
courage breaks the lines
the lines embrace in the sealight
nothing redeemed, unredeemed
stark manes from the stars

SEIZURES

    1

abut were we insectoid
the fraying trench & divot, national leaders, storm petrel
bugged, the 1980s
a fit from this compromise

I found a scrap of banner speak I wouldn't risk
RMT to wightlike, slate

you didn't meet a train through London corridors of the overworked

2

can never be precious with poems
or stay still long, apportioned place, broke up
engineer, a laggard

we wanted out of this light pollutant, we
were really toiling

minotaur skies over Hola, dilbit, Dresden

and day-dagger does for me
commuted, the fashionable ones forgotten
natal means shedding fathers

as a kid I ran through the countryside setting fire to footpaths
trusted almost everyone

so now I climb inside the washing machine & switch myself off

3

this morning it feels like we only have passions

you can apply for 79 jobs if you like

my uncle acknowledges, 'I shovel shit for a living'
while the poet graduates
into a paradise of debt & splendour
this basic disgrace

a hack life on top of a pile of prizes & abolishable university posts waits for you
it's there if you want it, sorted

last known let cosmic flame from a short-term star

or shapeshifting, manure, camouflage
auto-imposed
tread the sound

I need you to take my lines towards the others

4

friends steered into ditches, coops
strangers into ditches, coops

the best teachers aren't often the ones that know it

you have to listen carefully to them

5

now I prepare a small patch of ground

see no lyricists
becoming glacially monumental
official torturers, maiden voyages
that's from your defiance

the extraction of cobalt offered as a reason to have children
Divine Right of Delivery, summarily
greet me at my window

or the beloveds in the old painting flying over Vitebsk
although they can't look ahead

where Darwish is unauthorised to celebrate what he loves

all through the power surge, then
through the meltwater

Hanf's self-portrait
outlasts

and will outlast
the settlements of devastation

I greet you at my window

6

sometimes there's barely any music

priority boarding as the entire condition
Burley & Morgan caricatures

the lang pileup I shattered in my vindictive sleep
cram of
form with form, to write off their havens, polish, compound

when streaming has cushioned publics
the blonde ferryman stamps a passport

we're in Lost & Found
responsible to ourselves, in cavernous parks
or down the uneven pavement that passes by a securitised supermarket
tags for fucking cheese

'Beauty is a practice,' writes Christina Sharpe
and 'beauty shocks'

poetry can go on
you must waste every lock

7

yoked spiritually to 24-hour news

but looking for each other in the grimy half-light
crawling out of sewers & hiding places

strikers, disappointments, discarded souls

I witnessed an expensive mass of unrecognisable food, the world bolus
stunk of natural wine
space open for villagisation

how a poem counter-journeys through dispersed murder

how a livelihood flogs itself from the inside out
we demand a sinuous structure to think under it

8

little shoplift song
across bliss, attrition combat, GB
pleb debris

the essential hollowness in the existences of the rich

my rabbit warren
until there's nothing left to possess

in Aldi or Toppings
a tote bag's actually your secret comrade

9

and how was I still here, seeing you in that much pain from work
just about killed me, it kills me every day

snow from fire from fire from snow

I promise when the war for water comes

defeatists who deserted their poems
who can only talk about themselves
the limits of ressentiment
a poise to stall this poison

I will never not stand next to you

10

what's there now? jammed
years strung out in a sentence

my phrases, notations, falling as shades above the Priobskoye field

ringfenced with comments from marionettes of state
linkboy to New Town hoard

or beneath the shined shoes, enthroned, causal

will-o'-the-wisp running out of the wilderness

11

so we travel together under an intense wind
sweat on our backs, our mouths dry

a poem not for 'the universe', but right here
among houses & scorned trees
in the arms of other people

towards what refuses demolition

VIEWLESS

Grieves are the must points
among negative star tuck, ranging

That poets, like animals, are
dripping in their origin & elements, early ears
      to wraparound weather pattern~
lined donkeys, wasteful   heads over wire.

A secret knuckle isnt useful in the glass
and all days know a crossroads, turned to vinegar
with everywhere you look figures burst into silver scalpels
      seeing all the way out to hone horizon
'far on without chart'   or fullmoon
thought, washing in the hinterland

Honey hold of late-branch
and tuned to the method to insist like a slash
      lyre~ strung grit & soldering iron

Make heartbreak your music
Bar burrow through fire.

COUPON

And then at the end of it all I have this poem.
A phone mast thrown
           historically in the
node of Ranvier. It's a damaging doss,
spited flow, barged away   in knots where blue utopia steals
nil wing is redeemed.
What I've been at this year, cut through a kite depression dust
where devices never seen
follow us further into feudal mountains
              precast concrete
moral abeyance & aspic. Wise up. There are
flashes from spent objects, a mulctuary sprite
sea burr is how we take it
           struggling to echolocate across a
stopgap gully, their midair, our noncompliance
as health service waiting lists   cognitive spurs
produce a supple customer
the European forecast future gouges for
                    Boss, boss

A frond then I'm shaken. Swallow spears
outlive the inundating   house of this all
tilt play through a combat cloud
through a vice-chancellor's bonus, right honourable a geranium
and this cache of ancient
           pond scum due
ICI compensation
Your exhibit deserts us, alle farben,   brush of stuff killed 'literature'—
a petal toll, killed my holding tune
glassy endless with the privately educated
poems how to scrap together
              or blossom solvent
you were right and
so much more than scarecrows said.

Wince speech
unnerve what you know must be answered. This stance
one way I left my perch   what we found to light up
was time bent in the guttering, emission spine

that's debt for my head, from the gritstone plateau
I meant it. A word shone. At rest, or
rolling in ruin-nettle of Brock Mill
my collapse gives no one back,   the Ministry of Defence
Clyde water warheads
      to the north-west.

Too plain. Are you all there now. Do you talk Ward's
Stone. They won't find what it conceals. Wind belts our faces
aerial vehicle-scalp
cutthroat the method of a century
     bare in
coiled sadism of sane writers   calmly doing their jobs
     standstill of a tor breath
with a twist   of grease style & Twaron
luck mural to sleeper beaks
crossing & spinning   punctures of base lights
that look to go somewhere, bunker ring
foxhole flat, feather twitch. Hear accents leak property
editors emperors in the troposphere
    children of the rich & hungry.

What else breaks through on the meeting link, mayor-statements
would have chaff song work like a shock absorber
    or ending in a tent
inside for so long they destroyed their own
Am I tame or finchbrained
     in love with my own honey bruise
that it renders tip descriptive,   there's this slap
to sent creation, unfussed or the quick
Lune. Interrupting our own time
our own glances, pinch, a poem is a feud
   is the no-fly
     choral intercept, murder wiring the sky.

AFTER AND BEFORE

volatile vase-weapons, market worship
worsted   corrie luged with light bolt

an obsessive edifice to cruelty
'questing after knowledge'
                      and a loveless life

where my cursed wish went, so blood half
haloes   rabies, crowns ripped down & pissed on

                                          exiting the pawnshop
to do other than coldconstruct an effigy of mute mutilation
but vole move it

not searching for more killers than there are outside

not to crave choir-deputies
a mauve violin
or turn remote hedged dragon, cutting anyone away who will not wash & serve
        your highway or your highway   splits

this pro-doll with a tyrant's argument emerging from a rabbithole
I prefer poetry to be a little stupid on everything too.

tor telepathic attack from seven sides, medications
the replacement theorist
held a poisoning
barrow-banner that wants you only   on your own
                flutters over able ranks

in election season
these futures unlashing us slower than that
      so I've leapt at the writing them anyway.

from a longabused line of
            the part raving   tarred tapeworms, my lovers

to co-grasp
chartreuse whorl   we dont say

a ditchs trodden glint gift
clouding under the left ladder
                    told you may not ask for help you must beg

CHANGING THE GUARDS

verdicts invert, sleek light solos
                          to release a senseless heel
for the marl master
ducked window
watching people go to the polling booth illusion
     I flow to, my head on cold fire

         now the music points up
stranger, willow swallow a wart
in hearing distance of the world hitting
but not as rapid ruthless as it yet

once night tethers turn nooses
     I'll rearrange my stem cells

fell first needing to be less malicious than what reigns above
stormer aspirants   patio putty
don't become their monster
                    by what was, is done to us

                whoop err in the lit gases
ur-shattering fumeless statuary. the sworn
tale take of
to row now more a
sailing as a
        water dance of loons

SONG: EMISSIONS CAP

nettles fletched
under a travel
corridor

the gun hutch
ragwort
violet trough and through

desiring a flag
lyric a stave
burning in turbulence

what will you tell
to the mortals
who come after?

this is the close of the pig

INTERREGNUM

nobody's there, or
grips the fake light, or's held in place
by massive solar winds, each sibling severed
from a windmill like a cloudy headquarters
stockpiling fire
conspiracy to cause gullet flowers
the nightingale is alive

every last scrap of you pulls away from the sediment
a holly diadem
the personal skyscraper
moving you with its mind, same
thought at the same time, scrunched up
in the back lanes of a resilient violence
you mostly don't know how to even begin to
antiwrench, beech
leaf disease & blunt force charisma
over the hill teeth
a citizen approaches, you could denounce this all

when a dying animal
tries to be beautiful, in the disfiguring landscape
I can't think it's some kind of lie
turning from a bullshit order
to be marked by the oil spill & only the oil spill
the climate of nominated facts
these convulsions
but polishing a shield, caching a nut for shadows
we are the lowest minute scandal
slow-stolen fern off the zither, in
the way thorns feint
'a threat to life & property'
this property, this life

MY SHADOW

So we materialised too late. Field-bit music
splinters in sniffing weather   selfishness
        dressed up as free will

I saw an afterimage of Sky Plaza or the Gherkin
                  gleaming over your hired homes
inaccessible in one of the revamped CCTV cores of the world
where everything is geared to destroy

And reality   taking a shunned slice off
to write for the dead heralds, no hymns left to fuck up
pawing at our graves

       Don't talk about 'reality'
don't mention the fatal mildness in the air this month
doing my head in   returned angelical to seller

towards the full force of a meaning
reckless & deranged   who gives one
I count perverse blessings
     lain-low hubcap
           robin's bled detonator
bonfire turf

How will you know it's me at the window.
         So much is revealed by poetry
baked tree or Jenny Greenteeth
lurch screaming between visions
     a brutal arctic feeling inside
mannequin on the news   didn't call the truth

my lifetime gagged & mossed
         as I cut through Revoe Park from state horses
   mix knocks like a wrench.

Snipe to agile angles
blowing rapidly over the trapdoor
         stiff a long game
     jawbone composed of microplastics

    manic thought   that follows us out of the darkroom
                                        looking after baccy
animal offensives
ones you showed me
                not extinguished   stashed

It's my ditch
mood like an English zombie in the scheme of selective outrage
                and texts from Hermes
the divine presences are wicks   cold angst
deteriorating into a high temperature
                a thousand points of dismal shite
      for the focus group to focus on
                          names, labelknots erupt

Why would I beeline respectably   fess
for the cesspit, slick of a laundering light

All saints & all devils
                      beating the bounds
then carried along the Acheron
              in cairn language of the most recent data for all nations

Whats actually killing us
If I try and get some sleep
                    a clawed foot presses down on my forehead.

See silt east   lapwing gab & bow.
      Haze round Anglezarke or don't
                    accumulated household waste
          sign us off for 28 days
piss on the uni, wreck the fresco
bold like   ill brilliant sky unpicking
giving my slivers to you

        It gets harder & stranger to write this.
Pit earth has almost disappeared.
    Because nothing is safe
                so nothings predicted
Neighbourhood bill
rush to warble   or what remains
          of a blunt dart
in crowd surge of events
         we think flinging our questions outward
  removal centres

debtors & bluffs
        the last days of petrogovernance
handle it dented
                              feel it ending

I pull up out of chaos which shoves me at the robbed future
where history dies as a shoal

shot at coping   fractures on policy decisions
irresponsible songbird
                but better than the measure of treading water
in a gated community
                              passive aggression on tap
secretive drone whine   or resting against
grim torpor of a farmed style
                        so what

                It's not the time, it's not time yet
and before too long   youre in the ground.
Repetition
unbright bray of conjuring   cooking tribute
transfigured into boundless deferral

                      gets us hoovered up
with fellowship paramilitaries
collecting early coins
            that now the muzzle comes off

Blue mower tall-tells you how
a thing only exists if it's been used
or will be used soon
            burl bailiff dominion
winter vacantly   sickening a tight chest
to hate and to hold
            from this halfsecond forward
in resentment's bagged climate
can you forgive yourself

Sunup pill
                      puritan leaf brim
'a disordered devotion towards the real'
after redemption buried us alive
for vernal oracular
            not hanging from the ceiling
going lope past the tannoy   butcher

        & curtilage
                slow wage in dirt

But I'm one of the poets aren't I
                I'll do what I want
nothing a relic or
employment record   would strongarm me into
          Documents quivering
freefall through space
What do you fucking expect us to say
under palls that corrode   Grind pharynx
is a thorn
cocky I'd wind otherwise
                than a breezeblock line

The scum deep bucks about. There is
        still time. Coercive
payslip sovereignty   streams out of portholes
          nonfungible shrapnel
every burnt day
the knowledge
              that we can never let them get away with this

     my plover slurry   immune cloud rail
my bleach injection
but battering into a tempo
          from civil war permafrost
scorched in an electrical fire
            absolutely gone

What more for the auditors
            I havent got much left.
      Your face through exhaustion
          your sheet aluminium
                the poems that deserted us
writers with massive houses   pulling off heads

I crouch among the abandoned & meant.

FIRST NETTLES

life side, loved children leave the public squall
    square.
no buds but in weeds.   a newt recluse/ what now

poetry remained. no
passive fragrance,
        empires final sacraments

some assassin diagram   off light dry land.

at stanah
    past wastewater works
the reed's
late tsk. blurry

its ersatz shadow, second shell
backed away from   in a curt corner
    old bled world went
whybird. unoblivion. got. glowed

screw *social skills* of a
          twisting foil

on the loudspeaker   woid-woid
just somersault day is announced

      I also betray my depending pall

INSTEAD OF SLEEP

where I tack no lack
life overtook me, leap strafe

it's the ginnel of night   stars flute near my shoulder

in whip of a timesheet
I give what I have to the poems   that theyll move prey mess
      maybe for some listening friends
            or others over arc way I don't know

green knife lap
pissed   to velvet thistle
         here I love how the sky darkens & changes, sound
leading me from irrelevant speech
                in slur range
freed up past spite   I address you
with tattered weeds, whorl pitch
            I love how the language slaps me

too much of our writing
clocked   or collateral,
self-laceration
mimics algorithm culture
      the work society   not what we could throat on

           to turn from this thats slowly consuming you
I take an arrow from each

       winter breaches
and go outside of myself   not lost
         glamour of the undertow

frost is sword light

CROWN SHYNESS

       Through many a listening chamber
          —Percy Shelley

Death describes death.
Your swift wings it over blocks of flats   cutter updraughts
slew scout elbowed
      flouting almost everything
apart from the mozzies
anticoagulants   no duty
but our shriek musik, sree ree
        a premonition of summer curses
                  nauseous cacophony of 'La Marseillaise'
target above target
and in the subtle repositioning of trees
Birnam Wood
                skulks pickaxe
coolly
off to Dunsinane.
        I'm on the train now, out of a bad fever
60 quid return from capital to capital
bought months in advance   six hours' pay
midrib heat exhaustion
    thinking runup self-absorbed
            about the stagger, careening of my stuff
over the last four years
since we met
      undrowned
         in this horrific nationstate of
wholesale birdlime
from practical jokes   arch portals
          to vulpine rhyming
depression-dissension
glossa responsibility
      and what it was for
           whether anyone was altered completely
even at all
in a long descent
      could it mess me up, different

from that scatty silt & his emails
forced to put pressure   on binned violets
                and all the mistakes in between, trying bits
spooking the Bunsen burner
                                        riding out drudge doomed doubt
in spirals. The poem's not a windmill, that simply rapacious
never was
        or a bighead pulpit, or pestle & mortar
though I'm fucking pulverised when I get to the other side
if it's a great one   there's
no stolen lozenge, and
                anyway youd rather look at the sunrise, drastic fuchsia
the north-west seaboard
gorse torching
                                tune in a breadknife blue
real July bangers
wild combinations of fuckwit dulse & kelp
        kitty alone
                kitty awake
to watch a thief's sea squill
            from dune onus
                    cuckooing   This time
corrupt life
shunts back to go forward.

Cook or freeze. I reckon youve rattled them
being remembered was never important
                    ego's the joined up chasm
where crosscountry heatwave
                feels unimaginable
always a hostage environment
            unimaginable as *writing what we have to*
beautiful not ineffectual   in that old quarry
welkin bletting
                        so on earth I traipse across town
to hunt for a gas regulator
through intensifying temperatures
                while you hold the book table
                            envisioning another place
And this is what its like to never be satisfied
                design was costumes
spite locked in
            and wit like gauze & furze
too mesmerised with struggling
                endurance as valour

                                        we forgot to scrawl out to something
a dawn blot drawn from
                    infinitesimal torture
          each gliding scale   every capsized playtime
                                             churl on strike again
to the warm North Sea's tendon
                    caught, taped between tendencies
When professors shit talked 'the lyric'
in journals & the broadsheets
          which was just their own reified
                                        scarecrow idea of it
really it was whatever the hell you wanted it to be
                    a needed trigger, right Mau
the device you could do with
closest at hand   improvved
                    elastic as day tar
sunflower dextrous a pill to follow
in rancid advertising
          those famous speeches about privilege
                                        divide & incur
begin to sound hollow in the mouth of a dud
                    who cooperates with police   no atmos
or any middleclass tosser
                    throwing their weight around

40 degrees at Heathrow is murder.
 What does it mean to even have to come out with a sentence like that
                              whove I become
If we'd just skirl through the heat   mower to shimmer
                    binding & changing
                                        at the disposable BBQ
explosive drenching manoeuvre
lunar buck blasts Fountain Park
                                   I've needed adze of caw abstraction
both of you, spring-loyal   new grass
and eye to autumn when it's milder
with wouldbe heroes   petrified
                                        desiccated by technology
                    a rag blowing on a pole
niche breezes
          living 'rent free'
nowhere on the melt of the earth
balladry of aggression, mimicry
                              mortifications dialect
          our weak boneidle theme

                                                            to flush sky tint
                        a poet & a poets sad rules
mauled lucid dreams   sweating in joggers.
But some people barely bother to read do they
            piling into their inertia
                        the myth of the citizen
        an allegiance with translucence, deuces
sets your resting vow   hung in an open blush
                though megatons of the bomb
keen from this pinned bottle
            shatter my spirit & frame
                        and I'm burned alive
by fireclouds, culture secretaries
banish these lines
                from the citys hateful bounds
muttering to ourselves in a charred attic
        that chorus upends   quill quench
                                        and landscapes whirl

I'm here now listening. There's 'too much
talk in the world'   much less quiet relation
        beak nudge   fur in topsoil
                        even as I skitter across the blank iceshelf space.
Even as unripe berries fall
        from the whitebeam I'm shading under.
Their world is a lie. And
one that must be utterly transformed.
                A ballerina in stupendous lamplight   O pinion.
                        Listen to anyone hungry, to
            cleaners,
                        to the jobless, listen
        to the fucking killed, to whoever
            breaks their minds & backs for fuck all
and dont stop there but let yourself be translated
      with the people you love massively & adore, a devil's bird
            unwending uncursing the fabric future fighting
                        don't end
              with everyone in misery, chronic pain & suffocated
not in the way the lords & masters want
                    the gym or some trim & coat
keep buying crap or we're all done for
but the physics of this song I'm knitting, reaping on the wing
                    even when we die
          are turned away forever
                there'll be a rush of starting magical happiness

```
                                in knowing what we did do
though the remake tanks
                        though there was & is, can be
        no Eden anywhere else
                                no eyrie to speak of
                but on this ground, in this air
                                we're all we've got
as everything flashes up                    going down into the waves
            rosy stun of sun to moon
                        so my days werent only a disaster
and we may be there together
                        the scree of this
                                                        sree ree
```

INDEX OF TITLES AND FIRST LINES

    abut were we insectoid   104
A Dedication for Trench Foot   31
After and Before   118
A History of Birdsong   51
    a horse-dart over the silo leads   19
    All over the scar water, shaped ex-   29
    an animal wrote this. the blue debtor   101
    an arrangement that modernises us into passive dogs   61
    And then at the end of it all I have this poem.   116
    Anubis the jackal.   flashing halter on a fined sea-sky   58
A Salamander   90
    a torrent skip to talk on sleek   95
    a twist of the syllable, the billed spirit   21
Aureole   103

    blood and tonic, whiplash dashing   91

Castor and Pollux   63
Changing the Guards   120
    Circling the square   it flick spoke like struck me   41
    coarse stars   and the tongue sea   55
Cockatrices and Echoes   67
Comfort Zone   17
Coupon   116
Crown Shyness   129
Crude Thoughts   87

    Death describes death.   129
Decade of Innards   35
    deep memory   33
Doing Numbers   40

Fashionably Late   26
First Nettles   127
    flute inside how to not die down slowly   38
For Mau   14
For the Ones that Care   52

    gamut-wings   94
    Getting it down over a quack November night, the 16th   60
Giving Back   61
Go on Then   19
    Grieves are the must points   115

    hard to write a draught excluder, hard to stop   74
Hedge Accentor   38
Herne the Hunter   79
Human Factors   68

Hymn from Careers 81

  I keep green wits about me 22
  I'll leave, but loudly I'll leave 87
I Love to Walk the Fields 101
Instead of Sleep 128
Interregnum 122
In the Scratching Shed 22
  It was a dream of writing. News grazed the world, fires 63
  I woke up and the earth was still there. 36

  June wooze 28

  last defiance is a deep landscape so my hearers taught me 20
  left the openair bathhouse sauna to sand martin 17
  life side, loved children leave the public squall 127
Link Rot 27
  listen to the falconet haar-fold 14
Lug Poem 73

Market Psychology 58
Misrule 41
  Mite time's leaked twilight 70
  Move on the hinge. You think a composer 27
Muck for May Day 94
My Shadow 123

  nettles fletched 121
  Never a night as flawless as it is out here 52
  nobody's there, or 122
  Now poems feel 90

Ode to Spit 98

  painkillers. a revenue cloud. green foyer 62
Parole 33
Paroxysm: A Strain 49
Patent 55
Plaque's Heap 70
  poetry sled out 50
  Postures not hunted 67
Purgatory for Angels 36

  raked by silences 66
Reef Time from Tim's Reading 20
Reply to Sam After the Heatwave 29
Rufford Park Poachers 56

Seizures 104
  slip leaf blower 73
  so at first light there'll be a curve 40
Song: Emissions Cap 121
Song: Groundsel 21
Song: Lung Bud 57
Song: Mire Drum 66

Song: North Sea   16
    So we materialised too late. Field-bit music   123
State Funeral   69
    step inhumanly over the pavement   57

    temp sky   51
    that I stick on my hat down a slow street   103
    that there are gaps, crevices   68
    the back of the head   77
The End of Melancholia   91
    There's no good time to write   81
Thermal Storage   60
    The rockdove at the end of the palace coos   26
The Servant and the Stick   62
    the voices fall on my ears from all tight angles   31
    the water lily is   above your lease   56
    The wing is an anvil. Kevlar the sunset, existence   13
    The world will come after you   98
    This is the simplest poem   49

Unnumbed   77

    verdicts invert, sleek light solos   120
Viewless   115
Visual Snow   74
    volatile vase-weapons, market worship   118

Wandering Light   28
War Blur   75
    wasn't that l'histoire catamaran   79
Water and Armour   95
    well now I think I get what it's like to be ashamed   69
Went Whistle   50
    We swam to a source but it was no source   75
    where I tack no lack   128

Your Auspice   13
    your overseers won't leave you to your writing   35
    you've been a loner on the earth   16

ACKNOWLEDGEMENTS

Thanks to the editors of *Happy Birthday?*, *The Hythe*, *Blackbox Manifold*, *Kruk Book*, *Lana Turner*, *Shuddhashar*, *Spam*, and *Still Point* where some of the poems in this book or versions of them first appeared. Scraps were also printed on the inside covers of some issues of *Ludd Gang*, and I'm grateful to Gong Farm for making 'Seizures' into a pamphlet in 2022. Tom Crompton and Luke Roberts read drafts of most of the poems as they came along, and their responses and perceptions have been indispensable, the blazing weave of their poetry. I'm grateful to Sam Keogh for providing the stunning collage for the cover. Thank you as well to Phil Baber for his advice, insight and thoughtful work on this book: it wouldn't exist without him.

    A bunch of these poems were written for, to and with people who at some point or other walked around the same islands at the same 'time' as me. We spoke, ate and drank together, read to one another, poetry was our friend. This book is for all of them, in deep admiration of their writing and teaching. Their art gives me nerve. A few of the poems also had particular listeners in mind when I was putting them together. 'For Mau' is for Mau Baiocco. 'Reef Time from Tim's Reading' is for Robyn Skyrme. 'Wandering Light' is for Alex Marsh. 'Reply to Sam After the Heatwave' is for Sam Weselowski. 'Purgatory for Angels' is for James Goodwin. 'Hedge Accentor' is for Kyle Lovell. 'A History of Birdsong' is for Frances Kruk. 'Patent' is for Fred Carter. 'A Salamander' is for Andy Spragg. 'Water and Armour' is for Gloria Dawson. The 'Seizures' are for Sarona Abuaker, Tom Betteridge, Amy De'Ath, and Rob Kiely. 'Crown Shyness' is for Tom Crompton and Luke Roberts.

Copyright © 2025 by Dom Hale

Published by The Last Books, Amsterdam / Sofia

www.thelastbooks.org

Designed and typeset by Phil Baber

Typeset in Otto, designed by Sam de Groot
and Laura Opsomer Mironov

Cover artwork by Sam Keogh

Printed in the EU by Tallinn Book Printers

ISBN 978-9-49178-081-3